EXPLORING COUNTRIES

Cuba

by Walter Simmons

BELLWETHER MEDIA • MINNEAPOLIS, MN

Note to Librarians, Teachers, and Parents:

Blastoff! Readers are carefully developed by literacy experts and combine standards-based content with developmentally appropriate text.

Level 1 provides the most support through repetition of high-frequency words, light text, predictable sentence patterns, and strong visual support.

Level 2 offers early readers a bit more challenge through varied simple sentences, increased text load, and less repetition of high-frequency words.

Level 3 advances early-fluent readers toward fluency through increased text and concept load, less reliance on visuals, longer sentences, and more literary language.

Level 4 builds reading stamina by providing more text per page, increased use of punctuation, greater variation in sentence patterns, and increasingly challenging vocabulary.

Level 5 encourages children to move from "learning to read" to "reading to learn" by providing even more text, varied writing styles, and less familiar topics.

Whichever book is right for your reader, Blastoff! Readers are the perfect books to build confidence and encourage a love of reading that will last a lifetime!

This edition first published in 2011 by Bellwether Media, Inc.

No part of this publication may be reproduced in whole or in part without written permission of the publisher. For information regarding permission, write to Bellwether Media, Inc., Attention: Permissions Department, 5357 Penn Avenue South, Minneapolis, MN 55419.

Library of Congress Cataloging-in-Publication Data

Simmons, Walter (Walter G.)
  Cuba / by Walter Simmons.
    p. cm. – (Exploring countries) (Blastoff! readers)
  Summary: "Developed by literacy experts for students in grades three through seven, this book introduces young readers to the geography and culture of Cuba"–Provided by publisher.
  Includes bibliographical references and index.
  ISBN 978-1-60014-477-6 (hardcover : alk. paper)
  1. Cuba–Juvenile literature. I. Title.
F1758.5.S58 2010
972.91–dc22   2010011411

Printed in the United States of America, North Mankato, MN.

080110   1162

Contents

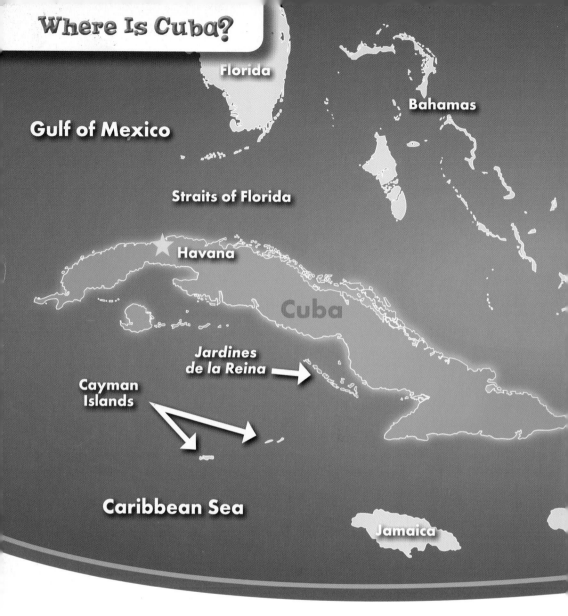

Florida

Gulf of Mexico

Bahamas

Straits of Florida

Havana

Cuba

Jardines de la Reina

Cayman Islands

Caribbean Sea

Jamaica

Cuba is an island nation that lies just 90 miles (145 kilometers) south of Florida. It is the largest island in the **Caribbean**. Cuba is 745 miles (1,199 kilometers) long and covers 42,803 square miles (110,860 square kilometers). Its seacoast winds for 2,321 miles (3,735 kilometers) around many bays and small harbors. Havana is the capital of Cuba.

Atlantic Ocean

Haiti

Dominican Republic

To the north of Cuba are the Straits of Florida, the Bahamas, and the Atlantic Ocean. Hispaniola is the island just east of Cuba. The nations of Haiti and the Dominican Republic share this island. Jamaica and the Cayman Islands are in the Caribbean Sea, which lies south of Cuba. The **Gulf** of Mexico splashes against Cuba's western coast.

5

Did you know?

Cuba's rain forests are much smaller than they used to be. For years, people have been cutting them down to make room for farmland.

Viñales Valley

Cuba has plains, **wetlands**, high mountains, and dense **rain forests**. A mountain range called the Cordillera de Guaniguanico rises over western Cuba. It gives way to limestone cliffs that tower over Viñales Valley. Forests cover the slopes of the Escambray Mountains in central Cuba. The highest peak in this range is Pico San Juan, with a height of 3,740 feet (1,140 meters).

The peaks of the Sierra Maestra in southeastern Cuba include Pico Turquino, or Turquoise Peak. At 6,496 feet (1,980 meters), it is the highest mountain in Cuba. The longest river in Cuba is the Rio Cauto. It begins in the Sierra Maestra and empties into the Caribbean Sea. Wetlands surround most of the rivers in Cuba.

Off the southwestern coast of Cuba is the *Isla de la Juventud*, or Isle of Youth. The name comes from the many schools that were built on the island for Cuba's children. The island has many Native American cave paintings that are hundreds of years old. Pirates once used this island as a home base. They knew it as *Isla de Tesoro*, or Treasure Island. Dozens of sunken ships surround the island, making it a popular spot for diving in search of buried treasure. The island is also famous for the *Presidio Modelo*. This prison once held 6,000 inmates. The prison is now a museum, and part of it has become a school.

Presidio Modelo

fun fact

The Spanish settlers of Cuba borrowed many words from the Taino people who already lived on the islands. The English words *barbecue*, *hammock*, *canoe*, and *hurricane* come from this Native American language.

Cuban crocodile

Cuba has hundreds of animals that cannot be found anywhere else on Earth. Dozens of wildlife reserves throughout the country protect these unique creatures. Between 3,000 and 6,000 Cuban crocodiles swim in the streams and freshwater pools of Cuba's wetlands. These crocodiles can leap 6 feet (1.8 meters) out of the water to catch a bird or other small animal.

Did you know?

Coral reefs line the southern coast of Cuba. Parrotfish, angelfish, and other tropical fish swim in and around the reefs to hide from sharks, dolphins, and other predators.

angelfish

Cuban hutia

Cuban bee hummingbird

In the rain forests, Cuban hutias look for food on the forest floor. These rodents are able to climb trees when predators like the Cuban boa constrictor come around. The Cuban bee hummingbird is the smallest bird in the world. It is just 2 inches (5 centimeters) long and weighs less than a penny. It shares the skies with the Cuban butterfly bat, one of the smallest bats in the world.

Over 11 million people live in Cuba. About 3 million Cubans live in and around Havana. Many Cubans have **ancestors** who were **colonists** from Spain. Some of these colonists married Taino people, the **native** people of Cuba.

Speak Spanish!

English	Spanish	How to say it
hello	hola	OH-lah
good-bye	adiós	ah-dee-OHS
yes	sí	SEE
no	no	NOH
please	por favor	POHR fah-VOR
thank you	gracias	GRAH-see-uhs
friend (male)	amigo	ah-MEE-goh
friend (female)	amiga	ah-MEE-gah

Did you know?
Over one million people born in Cuba now live in the United States, mainly in the city of Miami, Florida. To reach their new home, many risked a dangerous voyage across the Straits of Florida.

Some Cubans have ancestors from Africa. Their ancestors were brought to the islands as slaves to the colonists. Today, many Cubans have traits from all of these groups. Most people speak Spanish, which is the official language of Cuba. Some Cubans in the cities also speak English.

Did you know?

In Cuba, many people shop on the black market. They buy and sell goods outside of official government stores.

Cubans spend much of their time outdoors. They love to walk in the streets and talk with friends and neighbors. Most people use bicycles and buses to get around. It can be hard work to find food and other goods to buy. Many Cubans must search for hours to find the items they want. When they find a store with something useful, they often must wait in line for a long time.

Where People Live in Cuba

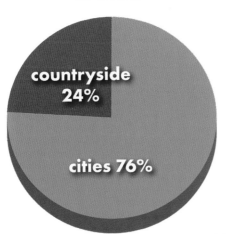

countryside 24%

cities 76%

To control the supply of food, the Cuban government **rations** it. At the end of the year, every family gets a ration book, which they call *la libreta*. The book tells them how much of each item they can buy every month. Rationed items include beans, rice, milk, coffee, soap, and sugar.

fun fact

Cubans sometimes get from place to place aboard a *camello*. This is a long trailer that looks like a bus, but it is attached to the back of a truck.

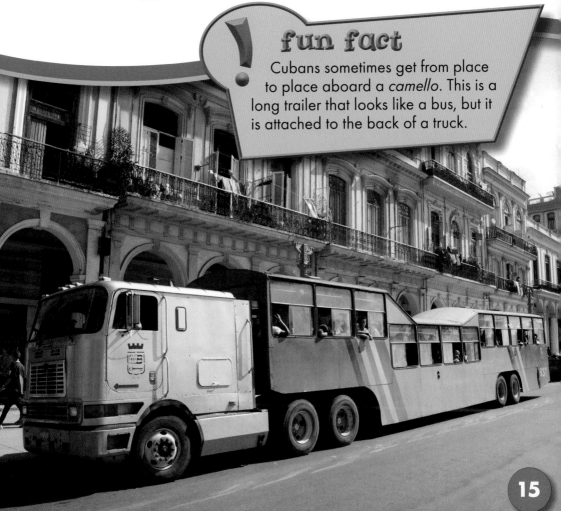

fun fact
Elementary school students wear white shirts, red pants or skirts, and scarves. In high school, students wear yellow pants or skirts. Students who go to medical school wear purple.

Cuba requires every child to go to school from ages 6 to 15. All students at every level of education wear uniforms. Students attend elementary school, the first level of education, for six years.

Then they move on to high school, which they must attend for at least three years. If they continue, students in their last few years of high school can focus on **technical work**, job training, or preparing for university. At university, students study teaching, medicine, and other subjects.

Where People Work in Cuba

manufacturing 19.4%

farming 20%

services 60.6%

fun fact

At one point, Cuba had as many cattle
as people. Today, beef is very scarce.
It is against the law in Cuba to kill
a cow for its meat.

The Cuban government promises every Cuban a job. However, not everyone gets a job, and many people can't find the jobs they want. Some people with college degrees wait tables at restaurants or drive taxis.

Cubans in cities work in banks, hospitals, schools, government offices, and other places. Some sell fruits and sandwiches at small stands along the sidewalks. Many of these stands also sell fresh fruit juices called *jugos*. In the countryside, farmers grow sugarcane, tobacco, and coffee on government farms. They also raise chickens, pigs, and dairy cows. Some farmers have small gardens where they grow their own food.

Cubans enjoy playing or watching sports and games. In the streets, Cubans of all ages play chess, cards, dice, and dominoes. Many Cubans love to watch boxing, which is a popular sport in Cuba.

Most Cuban kids play soccer, or *fútbol*. School soccer teams often play matches in city squares. Baseball, or *béisbol*, is another favorite sport. Cubans have been playing baseball almost as long as Americans. The first baseball championship in Cuba took place in 1878.

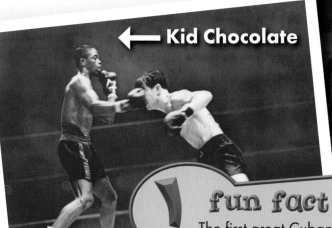

← **Kid Chocolate**

fun fact

The first great Cuban boxer was Kid Chocolate, also known as the Cuban Bon Bon. He was the first Cuban to ever win a world boxing championship.

Food

After eating lunch, Cubans rest for a few hours before returning to work. This midday nap is called a *siesta*.

Cuban food is hearty and filling. Most Cubans eat rice and black beans every day. Another common food is fried **plantains**. These look like bananas but have a salty taste. Cubans also love to eat chicken and pork. Roast pork is often served at parties and family gatherings. A favorite sandwich is sliced pork, ham, cheese, mustard, and pickles on Cuban bread. This is known around the world as the "Cuban sandwich."

Cubans enjoy a variety of desserts including ice cream and flan, a soft and creamy pudding. *Churros* are a popular treat made of fried dough sprinkled with sugar. Dessert is usually served with *café con leche*, or coffee with milk.

flan

plantains

fun fact

In Cuba, the government owns most restaurants. Private *paladares* are open in a few places. By law, these restaurants can only have 12 seats. They can't serve shrimp or lobster, which are reserved for government restaurants.

Cuba has several national holidays. Most of these celebrate the **revolution** led by Fidel Castro in the 1950s. Triumph of the Revolution takes place on January 1. It is a day to remember the success of the revolution that brought Fidel Castro to power. The following day, Cubans celebrate Victory of the Armed Forces Day. Late July has many holidays that celebrate the final events of the revolution. The time leading up to these days is called *Carnaval*. Huge parades wind up and down the streets of Havana. Fireworks light up the sky while people sing and dance.

Fidel Castro

Did you know?
Christmas was not a national holiday in Cuba from 1969 to 1997. It was made a national holiday again in 1998 in honor of a visit from the Pope.

The revolution in 1959 prevented Cubans from buying American cars. After the revolution, the United States put an **embargo** on Cuba. This meant that Cuba could no longer trade with the United States. Since there were no car factories in Cuba, nobody could buy a new car.

Cubans kept driving the cars they already had. They kept these 1950s models in good condition. They also converted the engines to use **diesel fuel**. This kind of fuel was easier to get in Cuba. About 60,000 cars from the 1950s still run in Cuba. The Cubans call them "Yank tanks," or *màquinas*. The old cars are symbols of Cuba's revolution and show Cuba's **resourcefulness** in tough times.

Fast Facts About Cuba

Cuba's Flag

Cuba's flag shows three horizontal stripes of blue and two of white. On the left side is a red triangle with a white, five-pointed star. Cuba officially adopted the flag in 1902, when the country won its independence from Spain.

Official Name: Republic of Cuba

Area: 42,803 square miles
(110,860 square kilometers);
Cuba is the 105th largest
country in the world.

Capital City:	Havana
Important Cities:	Santiago de Cuba, Camagüey, Holguín, Guantánamo
Population:	11,477,459 (July 2010)
Official Language:	Spanish
National Holiday:	Triumph of the Revolution (January 1)
Religions:	Christian (85%), Other (15%)
Major Industries:	farming, manufacturing, services, tourism
Natural Resources:	nickel, copper, salt, wood, oil, iron ore
Manufactured Products:	cigars, cement, machinery, medicine, oil
Farm Products:	citrus fruits, rice, sugarcane, tobacco, beans, plantains, yucca, coffee, cattle, pigs, chickens
Unit of Money:	Cuban peso; the peso is divided into 100 centavos.

Glossary

ancestors—relatives who lived long ago

Caribbean—the area west of the Atlantic Ocean and between North and South America; the Caribbean has many islands, including Cuba.

colonists—people who travel and conquer new lands for their home country

diesel fuel—a kind of fuel used throughout Cuba; diesel fuel is similar to gasoline.

embargo—an official order that stops one country from trading with another; the United States put an embargo on Cuba after Cuba's revolution.

gulf—part of an ocean or sea that extends into land

native—originally from a place

plantains—tropical fruits that look like bananas and have a salty taste; plantains are often eaten fried in Cuba.

rain forests—thick forests that receive a lot of rain

rations—sets limits on the amount of goods people can buy; the Cuban government rations food throughout Cuba.

resourcefulness—the ability to get through hard times and make the most of a situation

revolution—an uprising of people who change the form of their country's government

technical work—work involving machines and computers

wetlands—wet, spongy land; bogs, marshes, and swamps are wetlands.

To Learn More

AT THE LIBRARY

Green, Jen. *Cuba*. Washington, D.C.: National Geographic, 2007.

Hernández, Roger E. *Cuba*. Broomall, Penn.: Mason Crest Publishers, 2009.

Wright, David K. *Cuba*. New York, N.Y.: Children's Press, 2009.

ON THE WEB

Learning more about Cuba is as easy as 1, 2, 3.

1. Go to www.factsurfer.com.

2. Enter "Cuba" into the search box.

3. Click the "Surf" button and you will see a list of related Web sites.

With factsurfer.com, finding more information is just a click away.

Index

The images in this book are reproduced through courtesy of: Superstock Inc/Photolibrary, front cover; Maisei Raman, front cover (flag), p. 28; Juan Eppardo, pp. 4-5; Regien Paassen, pp. 6-7, 16; Danita Delimont/Alamy, pp. 8-9; Nik Wheeler/Alamy, p. 8 (small); Neil Lucas/Nature Picture Library, pp. 10-11; Stephan Kerkhos, p. 11 (top); Juan Martinez, pp. 11 (middle), 23 (left), 26-27; Lee Dalton/Alamy, p. 11 (bottom); TTL Images/Alamy, p. 13; Alex Fairweather/Alamy, p. 14; imagebroker/Alamy, p. 15; Getty Images, p. 17; Kevin Foy/Alamy, pp. 18, 24-25; Jose Luis Pelaez Inc./Photolibrary, p. 19 (left); Jeff Greenberg/Alamy, p. 19 (right); David Carton/Alamy, pp. 20-21; NY Daily News/Getty Images, p. 20 (small); Monkey Business Images, p. 22; Vinicius Tupinamba, p. 23 (right); Marka/Alamy, p. 24 (small); Jonathan Noden-Wilkinson, p. 29 (bill); Pablo H Caridad, p. 29 (coin).